SALT LAKE TEMPLE

Jennifer Howse

www.av2books.com

AV² provides enriched content that supplements and complements this book. Weigl's AV² books strive to create inspired learning and engage young minds in a total learning experience.

Your AV² Media Enhanced books come alive with...

Audio
Listen to sections of the book read aloud.

Key Words
Study vocabulary, and complete a matching word activity.

Video
Watch informative video clips.

Quizzes
Test your knowledge.

Go to **www.av2books.com,** and enter this book's unique code.

Embedded Weblinks
Gain additional information for research.

Slide Show
View images and captions, and prepare a presentation.

BOOK CODE

Y439434

Try This!
Complete activities and hands-on experiments.

... and much, much more!

AV² by Weigl brings you media enhanced books that support active learning.

Published by AV² by Weigl
350 5th Avenue, 59th Floor
New York, NY 10118
Websites: www.av2books.com   www.weigl.com

Library of Congress Cataloging-in-Publication Data
Howse, Jennifer, author.
  Salt Lake Temple / Jennifer Howse.
    pages cm -- (Houses of faith)
  Includes index.
ISBN 978-1-4896-1150-5 (hardcover : alk. paper) -- ISBN 978-1-4896-1151-2 (softcover : alk. paper) --
ISBN 978-1-4896-1152-9 (single user ebk.) -- ISBN 978-1-4896-1153-6 (multi user ebk.)
1. Salt Lake Temple. 2. Mormon temples. I. Title. II. Series: Houses of faith.
  BX8685.S353H69 2014
  726.509792'258--dc23
                    2014002104

Printed in the United States of America in North Mankato, Minnesota
1 2 3 4 5 6 7 8 9 0 18 17 16 15 14

032014
WEP150314

Editor: Heather Kissock
Design: Mandy Christiansen
Every reasonable effort has been made to trace ownership and to obtain permission to reprint copyright material. The publishers would be pleased to have any errors or omissions brought to their attention so that they may be corrected in subsequent printings. Weigl acknowledges Getty Images, Alamy, and Dreamstime as its primary image suppliers for this title. Page 12: Replica of altar by Robin Glassey © By Intellectual Reserve, Inc.; Replica of First Vision window by Sarah Neu © By Intellectual Reserve, Inc.; Replica of temple interior room by Sarah Neu © By Intellectual Reserve, Inc.; Page 13: Replica of baptismal font by Sarah Neu © By Intellectual Reserve Inc.

Contents

What Is the Salt Lake Temple?

Standing as the centerpiece of The Church of Jesus Christ of Latter-day Saints, Utah's Salt Lake Temple is a towering structure of grace. The building is an example of the amazing perseverance of the pioneers who designed and created this massive testament of religious devotion. It is the largest place of worship for followers of the Mormon faith.

During the 19th century, Joseph Smith founded The Church of Jesus Christ of Latter-day Saints in Fayette, New York. Even though it was a Christian religion, the Church had a unique belief system that other Christians had problems accepting. Followers moved often, trying to find a place where they could practice their faith freely.

By 1847, they found themselves in the area now known as Utah. Within four days of arriving, their new leader, Brigham Young, placed a stick where the temple was to be built. Six years later, he broke ground and laid the **cornerstones**. These stones marked the beginning of the Salt Lake Temple and the creation of a home base for the religion.

Construction of the Salt Lake Temple began on February 14, 1853.

The Mormon Faith

The Mormon faith is a Christian religion. This means it is based on the teachings of Jesus Christ, a man believed to have lived more than 2,000 years ago. Members of The Church of Jesus Christ of Latter-day Saints follow the teachings of two different books. One is the Bible, and the other is the Book of Mormon. The Book of Mormon supports the Bible and provides the Mormon view of Jesus Christ's teachings. Followers of the Mormon religion believe that the teachings of the Bible can be adapted to new ideas and situations. This is called continuous revelation. They also believe in an afterlife in which humans can become gods. The Church of Jesus Christ of Latter-day Saints is led by a group of elders, or living **prophets**. The head of the Church is called the president.

There are more than

140 Mormon temples
throughout the world.

15 million+
people belong to the Mormon Church worldwide.

More than 50 **percent** of these people live outside the United States.

The Mormon Church is the

FOURTH LARGEST
Christian Church in the United States.

Catholics
58 million+

Evangelical Protestants
50 million+

Mainstream Protestants
22 million+

Mormons
6 million+

A Step Back in Time

The Salt Lake Temple is based on an earlier temple Joseph Smith had built in Illinois. However, it also has several European influences in its design. Brigham Young, the leader of the project, lived in England between 1839 and 1841. His time there included visits to many of the country's iconic churches, such as Westminster Abbey and Worcester Cathedral. The structural design of these buildings made an impact on Young, and he incorporated many of their design features into the Salt Lake Temple. As a result, the temple has soaring **Gothic** towers and round **arches** reminiscent of the **Romanesque** style of architecture.

CONSTRUCTION TIMELINE

1847 Brigham Young marks the site of the future temple with a stick.

1858 Construction is temporarily halted when the U.S. Army arrives in the area.

1873 A railway line is laid between the **quarry** and the construction site. This allows rock to be brought to the site at a faster pace. Construction speeds up as a result.

1845   1850   1855   1860   1875

1853 The temple's ground-breaking ceremony is held in February, marking the beginning of construction. The cornerstones are laid two months later.

1855 The temple's **foundation** is completed.

1858 The original sandstone foundation begins to crack. The builders switch to quartz monzonite.

While style was important to Young, he also wanted the temple to stand as a symbol of Mormon strength and resilience. He had not forgotten the persecution the Mormon people faced before arriving in Utah. Young wanted a structure that would last a millennium. The building had to be tall and solid. It had to represent the people who built it.

London's Westminster Abbey is one of England's most important Gothic buildings. Known as the coronation church, it is where almost all of the country's monarchs have been crowned.

1885 The walls of the temple are completed.

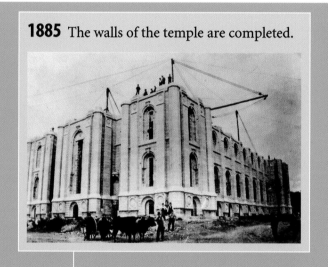

1962 The temple is closed for renovation. It reopens the following year.

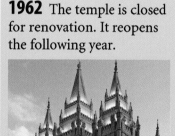

| 1880 | 1900 | 1950 | 1975 | 2000 |

1892 A **capstone** is placed on the temple to mark the near completion of the temple's exterior. Work continues on the interior.

1893 The Salt Lake Temple is completed, 40 years after construction began. A dedication ceremony is held on April 6.

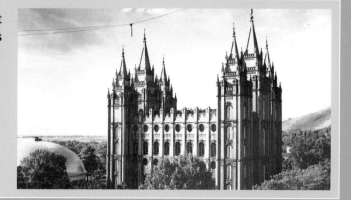

The Temple's Location

Today, the Salt Lake Temple is located in the heart of Salt Lake City, Utah's capital city. The temple is contained within Temple Square, an area that houses several buildings that are connected directly to church operations. Temple Square occupies 35 acres (14 hectares). The temple itself is found on the east side of the square.

HEIGHT The temple's highest point is the center **spire**, which extends 210 feet (64 meters) into the sky.

SURROUNDING WALL A 15-foot (4.6-m) high wall surrounds the temple.

The square serves as the city's core. Streets were planned in a **grid pattern** radiating out from Temple Square. This ensured the temple was at the center of the city and heart of the community. The streets were named according to their distance and position in relation to the temple.

AREA The temple site covers an area of 10 acres (4 ha). It has 253,000 square feet (23,505 square meters) of floor space.

★ Salt Lake City

UTAH

0   100 Miles
0   100 Kilometers

N

LENGTH AND WIDTH The length of the building is 186.5 feet (56.8 m). It is 118.5 feet (36.1 m) wide.

WALLS Each of the walls is 9 feet (2.7 m) thick at the base and 6 feet (1.8 m) thick at the top.

The temple sits close to several other key buildings in Temple Square, including the domed Salt Lake Tabernacle, and the Assembly Hall, which has spire much like the temple itself.

Touring the Exterior

The Salt Lake Temple was built as a symbol of the Mormon faith. Many of its design features relate directly to the beliefs of the Church and its members.

TOWERS Six towers rise from the temple. Four of the towers mark the building's four corners. Two tall center towers denote the front and back of the temple. The towers were built to represent the priests and bishops of the church. Each tower has 12 **pinnacles**, which represent other people important to the church. Inside each of the four corner towers is a spiral staircase made up of 172 steps. Each step is 6 feet (1.8 m) long and weighs 1,700 pounds (771 kilograms).

STATUE The center tower at the front of the temple is topped by a golden statue of the Angel Moroni. Mormons believe that the angel helped Joseph Smith locate and translate the Book of Mormon. The sculpture shows the angel blowing a horn, spreading the word of the gospel. The statue is made of copper and covered in gold leaf. It was created by artist Cyrus Dallin.

STONEWORK The temple's external walls contain several stones carved with symbols that have religious meaning to the Mormons. At the bottom of each **buttress** are earthstones, which represent Earth. Moonstones sit just above the earthstones. They indicate the stages of human life. Sunstones, cloudstones, and starstones are found higher on the temple walls. They represent the Mormon connection to the heavens.

The towers at the front of the temple are 6 feet (1.8 m) taller than those at the back.

The Angel Moroni wears a crown and a robe, signifying glory and righteousness.

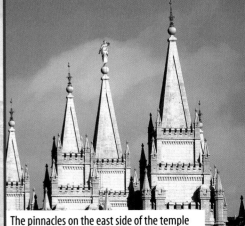

The pinnacles on the east side of the temple represent the Twelve Apostles of Jesus Christ.

A variety of statues surround the temple. Some portray founders of the Church. Others pay tribute to the pioneers who settled in the area.

The temple's doors have elaborately carved doorknobs, containing important symbols of the Mormon faith.

Engravings of clasped hands are found on each of the center towers. The hands symbolize fellowship, indicating that followers share a common purpose.

It cost **$3.5 MILLION** to build the Salt Lake Temple.

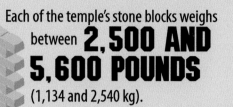

Each of the temple's stone blocks weighs between **2,500 AND 5,600 POUNDS** (1,134 and 2,540 kg).

The Salt Lake Temple has the **LARGEST** square footage of any Mormon temple.

THREE other temples were built in Utah before the Salt Lake Temple was completed.

The words *"House of the Lord"* are inscribed in gold on the front of the temple.

The temple sits on the highest point in Temple Square.

As many as 150 men worked on the temple's construction at any given time.

More than **2,000** people attended the temple's first dedication ceremony.

Touring the Interior

The interior of the temple continues the symbolism found on the exterior. Rooms inside the temple contain features that relay Mormon beliefs to the people who worship there.

ORDINANCE ROOMS People entering the temple pass through a series of ordinance rooms, where different teachings take place. Each room is decorated based upon a theme. These themes also give each room its name. People first enter the Creation Room, then the Garden Room, the World Room, and the Terrestrial Room. After leaving the final ordinance room, they enter the Celestial Room. This is the most sacred room in the temple.

SEALING ROOMS The temple features 14 sealing rooms. These rooms are used for ceremonies that unite people in marriage and confirm family relationships. Each sealing room contains an **altar** where the ceremony takes place. Mirrors on the walls symbolize that the sealing will last for eternity.

STAINED GLASS Several of the temple's rooms receive natural light through stained glass windows. The windows depict biblical symbols, floral patterns, and even the temple itself. The largest of these windows is called First Vision. It shows Joseph Smith meeting with God and Jesus Christ. The First Vision window measures 12 feet (3.7 m) in height. It was installed in 1892. Other windows were then commissioned for two of the sealing rooms. A fourth window, called the Memorial Window, was added to the temple after its dedication ceremony in 1893.

During sealing ceremonies, couples face each other on the altar.

Most Mormon temples have a stained glass window depicting the First Vision.

The Salt Lake Temple's visitor center has a model showing the temple's interior. The model allows people to see the temple's floor plan and what the rooms look like.

The Salt Lake Temple Visitor Center has a replica of the baptismal font found in the temple itself. Followers are baptized into the Mormon faith at the font.

The interior of the Salt Lake Temple was completed in **ONE YEAR.**

The Salt Lake Temple has **170** rooms.

An assembly room on the fourth floor can seat up to **2,200** people.

Only Mormons in **GOOD STANDING** are allowed to enter the temple.

ENTRANCE

Murals and reliefs inside the temple contain symbols of Church teachings.

A series of **tunnels** runs underneath the temple.

The Science behind the Temple

The construction of the Salt Lake Temple was an **engineering** feat that required careful planning for each phase of development. All elements of the building, including weight, height, and depth, had to be considered. Planners also had to ensure that the building would be safe and comfortable for Church members.

FOUNDATION The most important part of the construction design process was engineering a solid base. To ensure that the building remained stable, the temple's foundation had to support the weight of the building. The first foundation was made mainly of sandstone, which soon began to crack under the stress of the building it supported. The sandstone was replaced by large blocks of quartz monzonite that formed a 16-foot (5-m) wide by 16-foot (5-m) high base. The dense structure of quartz monzonite rock is durable and will not deteriorate. Packed tightly together, the rocks provide a solid base and limit movement of the building above.

ARCHES To further strengthen the foundation, its walls had inverted arches built into them. Arches work to redistribute weight. **Gravity** pulls the weight of a building downward, which can create excessive pressure on the foundation. An arch converts this downward force to an outward force. The outward force spreads the weight of the structure evenly across a larger area. Arches are found in other parts of the temple as well. Many of the windows sit inside archways. The downward force of gravity is redistributed here as well, helping the walls support the weight of the roof.

WIND Aside from resisting the force of gravity, the temple also must be able to withstand high winds. The statue of the Angel Moroni weighs 3 tons (2.7 metric tons) and stands more than 200 feet (61 m) above ground. At this height, it is vulnerable to high winds and could cause serious damage if it were to detach from the building. To ensure that this would not happen, it was important for the builders to firmly attach it to the tower below. They decided to secure a heavy weight to the statue's feet and let it hang inside the tower. Gravity pulls on the weight, which in turn pulls on the statue. This anchors the statue, but also allows it to sway and move with the wind. If it were to resist the force of the wind, it would likely topple.

The weight that anchors the Angel Moroni on the spire connects to the statue through the temple's capstone.

Although the foundation cannot be seen, it plays an instrumental role in supporting the temple's walls. This has allowed the temple to stand firmly in place for more than 150 years.

The temple's designers relied on scientific principles when building the window bays. They knew that each arch would support the stonework above it.

Salt Lake Temple Builders

Building the Salt Lake Temple required the efforts of many people. Mormons were committed to establishing a community in Utah that represented and supported their faith. The construction of a temple was an important part of developing this community, and most people wanted to help in some way. Skilled tradespeople worked alongside laborers to create a lasting symbol of their faith.

Brigham Young Brigham Young was born in Vermont in 1801, the ninth of 11 children. By the time he was 16 years old, he was working as an **apprentice** carpenter, painter, and **glazier**. Over time, he became a master carpenter, helping build several public service buildings, including a prison and the New York governor's home. In 1832, Young was baptized into the Mormon Church. He succeeded Joseph Smith as president in 1847, and was responsible for establishing the Church in Utah. When it came time to build a temple for the area, Young's experience in carpentry helped him design the building and supervise its construction.

Truman O. Angell Truman O. Angell was the main **architect** of the Salt Lake Temple. He was given the task of drawing the plans for the building that Young envisioned. Angell was born in Rhode Island in 1810. Like Young, Angell came from a large family and apprenticed to the trades at an early age. After joining the Mormon Church, he worked on the construction of at least two other temples before being assigned to the Salt Lake Temple. Angell did not live to see the temple completed. He died in 1887.

"Holiness to the Lord" plaques are now found on most Mormon temples. They serve to remind followers of the purpose of the temple and the respect it deserves.

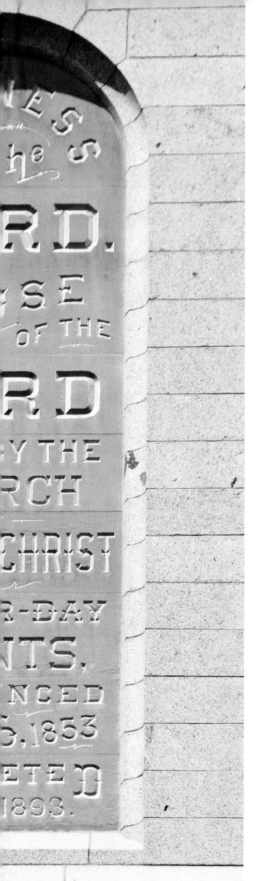

Truman Angell, Jr.

Truman Angell, Jr. Truman Angell, Jr. helped his father in much of the temple's planning, especially in his father's later years. Many of the masonry diagrams were drawn up by the younger Angell. He was also instrumental in adding a steam heating system to the building and redesigning the interior layout. This new layout expanded the ordinance rooms, and added a floor of offices and a large meeting room to the building.

Joseph Don Carlos Young Following the death of Truman O. Angell, Joseph Don Carlos Young was appointed as the new temple architect. Young was one of Brigham Young's sons and also one of the few trained architects in Utah at the time. He had received formal training as an engineer from New York State's Rensselaer Polytechnic Institute. Upon assuming his role as the temple architect, Young worked on implementing Truman Angell, Jr.'s revised layout and brought the project to its completion.

John Rowe Moyle John Rowe Moyle was one of the Salt Lake Temple's master **stonemasons**. He was born in 1808 in Cornwall, England. It was here that he learned his trade. Arriving in Utah in 1856, Moyle settled his family in the town of Alpine, a short distance away from Salt Lake City. He soon became involved in the construction of the Salt Lake Temple. As a master stonemason, Moyle made significant contributions to the temple. His best-known work includes the temple's circular staircase and the carving of the words "Holiness to the Lord" on the east exterior wall.

Similar Structures around the World

The Church of Jesus Christ of Latter-day Saints has grown considerably since its formation in the 1800s. Mormons and their temples can be found throughout the world. Some have been standing for more than a century. Others have been built to accommodate areas that have seen expanding congregations in recent years.

Nauvoo Temple

BUILT: 1999–2002
LOCATION: Nauvoo, Illinois
DESIGN: William Weeks
DESCRIPTION: The Mormon temple standing in Nauvoo, Illinois today is a recreation of the original temple, which was completed in 1840 but destroyed by fire eight years later. The temple was built in the **Greek Revival** style of architecture. This style is known for its use of columns. Nauvoo Temple has a series of rectangular columns running around its exterior walls. These columns make the building resemble a Greek temple.

The Nauvoo Temple is made of limestone that was brought in from Alabama. The original temple's limestone came from Illinois, but the quarry site was destroyed by flooding in 1912.

San Diego California Temple

BUILT: 1988–1993
LOCATION: San Diego, California
DESIGN: William S. Lewis, Jr., Dennis Hyndman, Shelly Hyndman
DESCRIPTION: Located high atop a hill in the San Diego community of La Jolla is one of the most striking Mormon temples. Two 190-foot (58-m) tall towers reach to the heavens, bracketing a star-shaped **atrium** and its gardens. The temple itself is composed of a series of **terraces** that add to its visual impact. Its gleaming white exterior finish is made from marble chips set in plaster. Lush gardens surround the temple, providing followers and members of the public with a place for quiet reflection.

The San Diego Temple cost almost $24 million to build.

The San Salvador El Salvador Temple's exterior walls are made from Brazilian granite.

San Salvador El Salvador Temple

BUILT: 2011
LOCATION: San Salvador, El Salvador
DESIGN: VCBO Architecture
DESCRIPTION: The San Salvador El Salvador Temple was the first Mormon temple to be built in El Salvador. The three-story building was designed with a Spanish influence and features several archways and **conches**. El Salvador's national flower, the *flor de izote* is on display in many of the temple's stained glass windows and woodwork. The temple has two ordinance rooms and two sealing rooms. A meeting house and housing complex stand next to the temple.

Issues Facing the Temple

Buildings deteriorate over time if proper **conservation** steps are not taken. All materials will break down, some faster than others. The builders of the Salt Lake Temple constructed a building that they hoped would last for 1,000 years. Followers of The Church of Jesus Christ of Latter-day Saints are doing what they can to ensure the temple remains in good condition for a long time.

WHAT IS THE ISSUE?

Some of the temple's electrical wiring is old and has been in the building for many years.	Metal light fixtures risk damage from exposure to the elements.	The large number of visitors to the temple puts a great deal of wear and tear on the hardwood floors.

EFFECTS

Faulty wiring may cause a short fuse. This can result in damage to lighting systems and electrical machines. There is also an increased chance of fire.	Dirt can slowly destroy the finish on brass lighting.	If the finish on a hardwood floor wears away, the wood itself can become pitted and begin to rot.

ACTION TAKEN

Electrical wiring is checked every year and repaired or replaced when necessary.	Metals, such as the brass on light fixtures, are delicately cleaned on a regular basis.	Hardwood floors in need of repair have their finish stripped and replaced.

Test an Inverted Arch

Arches are considered an effective way to distribute the weight of a building. They have been used in construction for centuries. The Salt Lake Temple relies on inverted arches to support the building's weight. Try this experiment to determine which type of arch will best hold a heavy load.

weights

Materials
- Three stackable weights, such as stones or metal weights, about 1 pound (0.5 kg) each
- Modeling clay
- 2 rectangular pieces of cardboard

modeling clay

Instructions

1. Place one piece of cardboard on a table.

2. Mold the clay into four arches that are narrow at the base and wide at the top. Place the four arches in a row on top of the cardboard. Place the arches close together so the tops are touching. This will create a base for your weights.

cardboard

3. Place the weights evenly along the top of the arches. Watch to see if your arches are able to support the weight.

4. Test the strength of the arches in different situations. For instance, slowly shake your cardboard base to simulate an earthquake. Watch to see if the arches are still able to support the heavy weights.

5. Now, create a new set of arches. This time, make them larger at the base and narrow at the top. Place them on the cardboard base, and then put the second piece of cardboard on top of the arches as a way to join them together. Place the weights on top of the new row of arches and watch to see if this type of arch can support the weight. Simulate another earthquake, and see what happens.

Compare your results to determine which form of arch provides the best support for heavy buildings.

Salt Lake Temple Quiz

Q Who founded The Church of Jesus Christ of Latter-day Saints?

A Joseph Smith

Q What are the two main architectural styles found in the Salt Lake Temple?

A Gothic and Romanesque

Q How many years did it take to build the Salt Lake Temple?

A 40 years

Q How many rooms does the Salt Lake Temple have?

A 170 rooms

Key Words

altar: an elevated structure where religious ceremonies are held

apprentice: a person who is learning a trade from a master

arches: curved structures that span an opening

architect: a person who designs buildings

atrium: an open area in a building, often containing plants

buttress: a support that projects out from a wall

capstone: the top stone on a structure

conches: smooth, concave surfaces that resemble the interior of a dome

conservation: the act of preventing damage or decay

cornerstones: stones at the corner of a wall, often the first stones laid in a structure

engineering: the application of scientific and mathematical principles to construct buildings and other structures

foundation: construction below the ground that distributes the load of a building or structure built on top of it

glazier: a person who cuts and fits glass

Gothic: a style of design that began in the 12th century

gravity: the force that pulls objects toward the center of Earth

Greek Revival: a style of design that is influenced by classical Greek architecture

grid pattern: a city plan in which the streets run at right angles to each other

pinnacles: small spires

prophets: people who deliver messages believed to come from God

quarry: a pit from which stone is obtained

Romanesque: a style of design influenced by Roman architecture

spire: a conical shaped feature that adds height to a building

stonemasons: people skilled in building with stone

terraces: a series of level platforms

Index

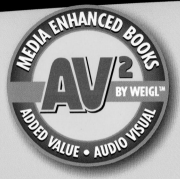

Log on to www.av2books.com

AV² by Weigl brings you media enhanced books that support active learning. Go to www.av2books.com, and enter the special code found on page 2 of this book. You will gain access to enriched and enhanced content that supplements and complements this book. Content includes video, audio, weblinks, quizzes, a slide show, and activities.

AV² Online Navigation

Book Pages
AV² pages directly correspond to pages in the book.

Audio
Listen to sections of the book read aloud.

Video
Watch informative video clips.

Embedded Weblinks
Gain additional information for research.

Key Words
Study vocabulary, and complete a matching word activity.

Quizzes
Test your knowledge.

Slide Show
View images and captions, and prepare a presentation.

Try This!
Complete activities and hands-on experiments.

AV² was built to bridge the gap between print and digital. We encourage you to tell us what you like and what you want to see in the future.

Sign up to be an AV² Ambassador at www.av2books.com/ambassador.

Due to the dynamic nature of the Internet, some of the URLs and activities provided as part of AV² by Weigl may have changed or ceased to exist. AV² by Weigl accepts no responsibility for any such changes. All media enhanced books are regularly monitored to update addresses and sites in a timely manner. Contact AV² by Weigl at 1-866-649-3445 or av2books@weigl.com with any questions, comments, or feedback.